THE EAGLE MOTHER

By Hetxw'ms Gyetxw (Brett D. Huson)
Illustrated by Natasha Donovan

HIGHWATER
PRESS

UNEXPECTED STORM

A strong wind blows through the valleys of Xsan, River of Mists. The land feels chilled and moisture carries the cold into every imaginable nook and cranny. The sun, which crested over the mountain during the early morning rain, now struggles to peek through an unexpected winter flurry.[1] The Gitxsan would say "gal 'nakwhl maadim," the winter is too long. This is the time of Lasa ya'a, the Spring Salmon's Returning Moon, the moon we see during the month of April.

Canada Council **Conseil des Arts**
for the Arts **du Canada**

We acknowledge the support of the Canada Council for the Arts.
Nous remercions le Conseil des arts du Canada de son soutien.

HighWater Press gratefully acknowledges the financial support of the Province of Manitoba through the Department of Sport, Culture and Heritage and the Manitoba Book Publishing Tax Credit, and the Government of Canada through the Canada Book Fund (CBF), for our publishing activities.

HighWater Press is an imprint of Portage & Main Press.
Printed and bound in Canada by Friesens
Design by Relish New Brand Experience
Cover Art by Natasha Donovan

Library and Archives Canada Cataloguing in Publication

Title: The Eagle Mother / by Hetxw'ms Gyetxw (Brett D. Huson) ; illustrated by Natasha Donovan.
Names: Huson, Brett D., author. | Donovan, Natasha, illustrator.
Description: Series statement: Mothers of Xsan
Identifiers: Canadiana (print) 20190169540 | Canadiana (ebook) 20190169567 | ISBN 9781553798590 (hardcover) | ISBN 9781553798606 (EPUB) | ISBN 9781553798613 (PDF)
Subjects: LCSH: Traditional ecological knowledge—British Columbia—Juvenile literature. | LCSH: Indigenous peoples—Ecology—British Columbia—Juvenile literature. | LCSH: Ecology—British Columbia—Juvenile literature. | CSH: Native peoples—Ecology—British Columbia—Juvenile literature.
Classification: LCC GN476.7 .H87 2020 | DDC j306.4/5097111—dc23

22 21 20 19   1 2 3 4 5

www.highwaterpress.com
Winnipeg, Manitoba
Treaty 1 Territory and homeland of the Métis Nation

Kispiox
River

Stekyodin

Bulkley
River

Skeena River

The Gitxsan

The Gitxsan Nation are Indigenous peoples from unceded territories in the Northwest Interior of British Columbia. This 35,000 square kilometres of land cradles the headwaters of Xsan or "the River of Mist," also known by its colonial name, the Skeena River. The land defines who they are.

The Nation follows a matrilineal line, and all rights, privileges, names, and stories come from the mothers. Lax Seel (Frog), Lax Gibuu (Wolf), Lax Skiik (Eagle), and Gisghaast (Fireweed) are the four clans of the people. It is taboo to marry a fellow clan member, even when there are no blood ties.

The four clans are divided among the territories by way of the Wilp system. A Wilp, or "house group," is a group comprising one or more families. Each Wilp has a head chief and wing chiefs, who are guided by Elders and members of their Wilp. Currently, there are 62 house groups, and each governs their portion of the Gitxsan Territories.

The Gitxsan Moons

K'uholxs	Stories and Feasting Moon	January
Lasa hu'mal	Cracking Cottonwood and Opening Trails Moon	February
Wihlaxs	Black Bear's Walking Moon	March
Lasa ya'a	Spring Salmon's Returning Home Moon	April
Lasa 'yanja	Budding Trees and Blooming Flowers Moon	May
Lasa maa'y	Gathering and Preparing Berries Moon	June
Lasa 'wiihun	Fisherman's Moon	July
Lasa lik'i'nxsw	Grizzly Bear's Moon	August
Lasa gangwiikw	Groundhog Hunting Moon	September
Lasa xsin laaxw	Catching-Lots-of-Trout Moon	October
Lasa gwineekxw	Getting-Used-to-Cold Moon	November
Lasa 'wiigwineekxw or Lasa gunkw' ats	Severe Snowstorms and Sharp Cold Moon	December
Ax wa	Shaman's Moon	a blue moon, which is a second full moon in a single month

¹ **Nitrogen** is a chemical element found in all living things. It is an important fertilizer for the Xsan ecosystem.

² An **ecosystem** is a community of living things together with their environment.

The world of the Gitxsan people does not exist without all the beings within their ecosystem, so the eagles will always be present. Nox X̲sgaak and her partner may use this same cottonwood for up to 20 years. The time they spend here not only benefits the cottonwood, but the nitrogen-rich[1] skin and bone they leave at the bottom of the tree decays and leaves nutrients to spread throughout the ecosystem.[2]

Much like the eagles, the Gitxsan depend on the salmon. They learn to fish from their mothers and fathers in the same way. Grandparents, parents, aunts, and uncles all do their part, teaching the young people how to spot the best run, when to fish, and how to catch this vital resource that not only helps them survive, but is an integral part of Gitxsan life and understanding of the world around them.

The siblings have a new perspective of the world below. With their eagle eyes, they see everything four to eight times farther and clearer than the best Gitxsan eyes. From above the trees, they watch a large black mass moving under the surface of Xsan. Their instinct drives them to dive to the water below to grab at the sockeye that swim beneath the rapids. A lack of experience leaves them unsuccessful, and they drop down beside the eagle mother to steal from her fresh catch.

A Final Run

August is here and Lasa lik'i'nxsw, the Grizzly Bear's Moon, has arrived. The Gitxsan people now spend their days down by the river, waiting for the schools of miso'o, sockeye salmon, to arrive. Sister has survived and is now larger than her brother. Nox X̲sgaak and her mate still offer sympathetic meals to the young eagles, but only for another week or so.

The eaglets will spend several more weeks completely dependent on Nox X̱sgaak and her mate. Then the young birds will fledge[1] and start branching around the nest. When the eagles are branching,[2] they are flapping their powerful new feathers in a dance that teaches them about their wings, giving them confidence and desire to take flight.

¹ Birds **fledge** when they grow the necessary feathers to fly.

² **Branching** means stepping out of the nest onto branches to flap their wings and test out their new feathers.

¹ **Persevering** means to continue trying to do something even though it is difficult.

The cottonwood is now covered in leaves, and on hot summer days, it provides shade to all who live around it. At the nest, which sits over a metre deep and nearly two metres wide, young eaglets wait impatiently for their next meal. Sister is small compared to her brother. Nature favours the strong and so does Nox Xsgaak. She has been feeding more to brother. But, in an environment that is both delicate and unforgiving, sister is persevering.[1] Father must see something the eagle mother does not. He has been feeding sister after his hunt. Although she is still smaller, she has grown too big for brother to kill or push out of the nest.

SIBLING RIVALRY

Lasa maa'y, the Berry Moon, is fast approaching, as we are now into the month of June. As the people along Xsan are harvesting berries to preserve for the long winter months, Nox Xsgaak and her mate are feverishly hunting to keep up with the demands of their two young eaglets.[1] The eagle mother's larger size allows her to carry more back to the nest in one trip.

[1] An **eaglet** is a young eagle.

¹ **Incubating** means to keep the eggs warm until they are ready to hatch.

As her mate arrives, Nox X̱sgaak moves to the edge
of the nest where she can finally shake the snow from
her feathers. Two large eggs are now exposed to light
and cold. The father hastily moves to take his turn at
incubating.[1] The eggs will hatch in about two weeks.
This mother and father will pair for life, and they
have been together now for three breeding
seasons. The spring storm hasn't dampened
their spirits, nor is it stopping the Gitxsan
from fishing along the riverbanks below.

Amongst the thick brush of the riverbank, t'uuts'xw am'mal, a black cottonwood, stretches high above the other trees. Woven into the fork of its strongest branches is the nest of Nox Xsgaak, the eagle mother. She appears frozen to the tree, but she is protecting an important treasure.

¹ A **flurry** is a brief, light snowfall.